BLACK TRAILBLAZERS IN SPORTS

VENUS AND SERENA WILLIAMS

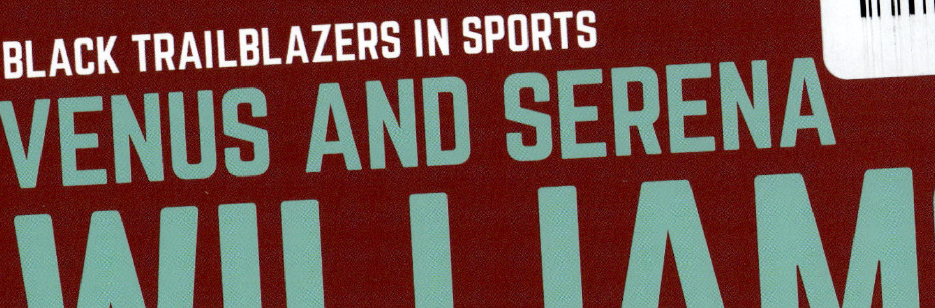

by David Lee Morgan Jr.

FOCUS READERS
NAVIGATOR

WWW.FOCUSREADERS.COM

Focus Readers is distributed by North Star Editions:
sales@northstareditions.com | 888-417-0195

Produced for Focus Readers by Red Line Editorial.

Photographs ©: Anja Niedringhaus/AP Images, cover, 1; Laurent Rebours/AP Images, 4–5; Jacques Demarthon/AFP/Getty Images, 7; Thomas Coex/AFP/Getty Images, 8; Ken Levine/Allsport/Getty Images Sport/Getty Images, 10–11; Paul Harris/Online USA/Getty Images Sport/Getty Images, 13; Al Bello/Getty Images Sport/Getty Images, 15; Thierry Orban/Sygma/Getty Images, 16–17; Clive Brunskill/Getty Images Sport/Getty Images, 18, 21; Shutterstock Images, 22–23, 26; Greg Allen/Invision/AP Images, 24; Red Line Editorial, 29

Library of Congress Cataloging-in-Publication Data
Names: Morgan, David Lee, author.
Title: Venus and Serena Williams / by David Lee Morgan, Jr.
Description: Mendota Heights, MN: Focus Readers, [2025] | Series: Black trailblazers in sports | Includes bibliographical references and index. | Audience: Grades 4-6
Identifiers: LCCN 2023053990 (print) | LCCN 2023053991 (ebook) | ISBN 9798889982159 (hardcover) | ISBN 9798889982715 (paperback) | ISBN 9798889983781 (pdf) | ISBN 9798889983279 (ebook)
Subjects: LCSH: Williams, Venus, 1980---Juvenile literature. | Williams, Serena, 1981---Juvenile literature. | African American women tennis players--Biography--Juvenile literature. | African American sisters--United States--Biography--Juvenile literature. | Women Olympic athletes--United States--Biography--Juvenile literature. | Wimbledon Championships--Juvenile literature. | Australian Open (Tennis tournament)--Juvenile literature. | Racism in sports--Juvenile literature. | Sexism in mass media--Juvenile literature. | Equal pay for equal work--Juvenile literature.
Classification: LCC GV994.A1 M665 2025 (print) | LCC GV994.A1 (ebook) | DDC 796.342092/52 [B]--dc23/eng/20231215
LC record available at https://lccn.loc.gov/2023053990
LC ebook record available at https://lccn.loc.gov/2023053991

Printed in the United States of America
Mankato, MN
082024

ABOUT THE AUTHOR

David Lee Morgan Jr. is the author of 11 books, including *LeBron James: The Rise of a Star* and *Breaking Through the Lines: The Marion Motley Story*. Morgan was a longtime sportswriter with the *Akron Beacon Journal* and is now a high school English teacher and public speaker.

TABLE OF CONTENTS

CHAPTER 1

DOUBLES CHAMPIONS

Venus and Serena Williams stepped onto the court at the French Open. It was June 1999, and the sisters were playing in their first major doubles championship. Venus was nearly 19 years old. Serena was only 17.

The Williams sisters faced Martina Hingis and Anna Kournikova. Hingis

Serena Williams (left) and Venus Williams play in the 1999 French Open.

was 18 at the time, and Kournikova was nearly 18. They were young, too. But they had more championship experience than Venus and Serena.

The odds were against the Williams sisters. Yet they were confident. Venus and Serena won the first set 6 games to 3. They looked as if they would cruise to victory. In the second set, they stormed out to a 5–1 lead. However, Hingis and Kournikova rallied. They came back to win the set 7–6. The match was now even heading to the third and final set.

That's when Venus started to get nervous. Her confidence was shaken. But she worked to refocus. She regained her

The French Open uses clay courts. Balls bounce higher and move slower on clay.

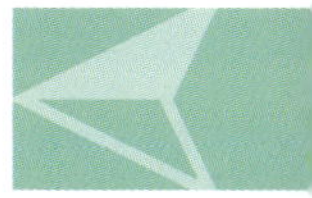

The Williams sisters hold the French Open trophy alongside Anna Kournikova and Martina Hingis (far right).

composure. The final set was close. The score went back and forth. Venus and Serena were ahead 7–6. In the next game, the Williams sisters won the first three points. With one more point, they would win the championship.

Kournikova served, and Venus returned. Then Kournikova hit the ball into the net. That was game, set, and match. Venus and Serena won the set 8–6. They became the first pair of sisters to win a **Grand Slam** tournament in more than 100 years. There would be many more victories to come.

SINGLES CHAMP

Later in 1999, Serena made a name for herself as a singles player. In September, she defeated Hingis to win the US Open title. Hingis was ranked No. 1 in the world at the time, and Serena was ranked No. 6. Serena won the match in straight sets. It was her first Grand Slam singles title.

CHAPTER 2

SISTERHOOD

Venus Williams was born on June 17, 1980, in Lynwood, California. Her younger sister, Serena Williams, was born on September 26, 1981, in Saginaw, Michigan. Their parents are Richard Williams and Oracene Price.

Richard and Oracene raised Venus and Serena in Compton, California. Richard

Venus enjoys her time with her father, Richard Williams, during a practice in 1990.

loved tennis. He watched videos and read books to learn more. Then he helped his wife learn how to play so they could teach their daughters.

Venus and Serena started playing in their neighborhood. The tennis courts were in poor shape. The neighborhood also had a lot of crime. They often heard police sirens when they practiced. Sometimes, broken bottles lay on the court. It wasn't the best place for Venus and Serena to practice.

However, the sisters didn't let those distractions bother them. They practiced hard and got better every day. Their work soon paid off. Both girls began

Richard practices with Serena in Compton in 1991.

winning tennis tournaments all around Southern California. Serena entered her first tournament before she was five. By the time she was nine, her record was 46–3. Meanwhile, 10-year-old Venus was blasting serves at more than 100 miles per hour (161 km/h). By 1991, she had a 63–0 record on the US junior tour.

However, both sisters faced **racism** at these tournaments. Tennis was still a mostly white sport. Partly for this reason, the girls' parents pulled them out of junior tennis in California. The family moved to West Palm Beach, Florida. Richard and Oracene wanted their daughters to attend a tennis academy. They also wanted both girls to work with Rick Macci, a famous tennis coach.

Venus and Serena continued to improve their game. The sisters even started receiving **endorsement** deals

In 1994, Venus played her first pro event at a tournament in Oakland, California.

from companies. And they weren't even teenagers yet. By 1994, Venus was ready to turn pro. She was just 14 years old. Serena went pro the next year.

CHAPTER 3

HITTING THE PRO CIRCUIT

Venus and Serena had dominated at the amateur level. They did the same on the professional **circuit**. Their style of play was remarkable. Both became known for their power, athleticism, and attacking mindset.

The sisters changed women's tennis in many ways. For example, serves did not

Venus Williams had one of the fastest serves in women's tennis. Serena's was just a bit slower.

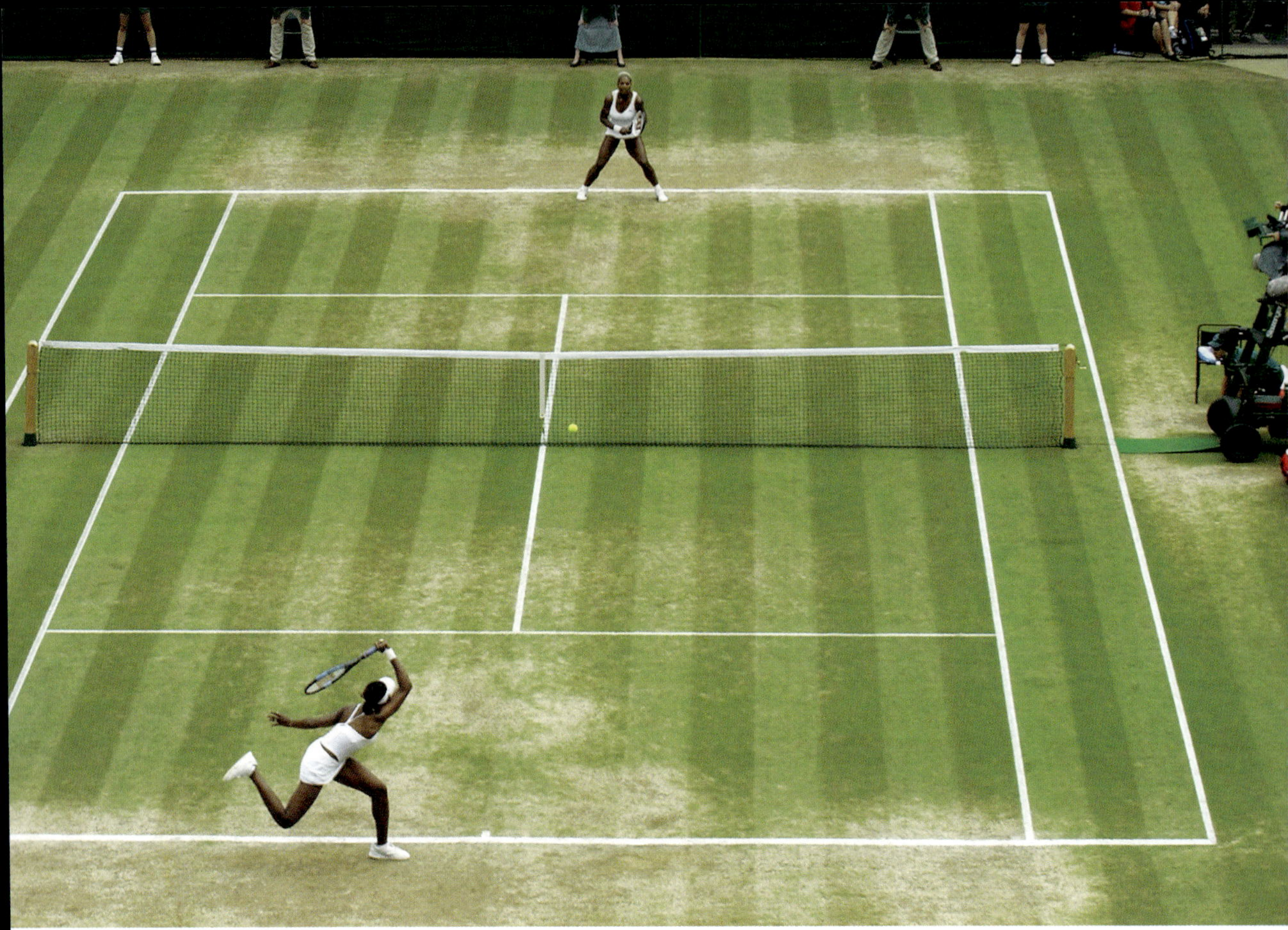

Venus (bottom) hits a forehand during the 2002 Wimbledon final against Serena (top).

usually give servers much advantage. But the Williams sisters' serves were strong and fast. They were perfectly placed, too. As a result, opponents often had trouble returning the sisters' serves.

In 2000, Venus won Wimbledon and the US Open. In 2001, she won them both again. Serena was close behind. In fact, she lost to Venus at the 2001 US Open Final. It was the first time they played each other in a Grand Slam final. It would not be the last. In 2002, the sisters faced off at three finals. Serena won all three. That year, both players spent time as the No. 1 player in the world.

In 2003, Serena faced Venus for the fourth straight major final. She defeated Venus at the Australian Open. Serena had just won all four Grand Slam tournaments in a row. This feat became known as the "Serena Slam."

Injuries soon impacted both sisters. But they managed to return to the top. They continued to win championships.

At the 2017 Australian Open, Venus and Serena met again in the final. Serena won. It marked Serena's 23rd major championship. At the time, that was the most of any man or woman in the **Open Era**. In addition, Serena was two months

NO. 1 IN DOUBLES

As a doubles team, Venus and Serena peaked in 2009 and 2010. They won four majors in a row over those two years. That made for another Serena Slam. Their victories launched Venus and Serena to the No. 1 ranking in doubles.

Serena returns a shot in the 2017 Australian Open Final against Venus.

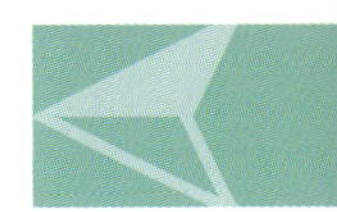

pregnant. She took time off after the Australian Open to have her baby. Months later, she was back on the court.

CHAPTER 4

LEGACY

Historically, tennis was a mostly white sport. It had many rules for female players. These rules said how to dress and act. They fit racist and **sexist** ideas about women. These ideas valued wealthy, white women who were quiet and less strong.

Venus and Serena Williams changed that. They were Black. They wore braids

Serena screams with passion after a big point during a match against Venus.

In 2018, an umpire penalized Serena for arguing a call. She said men are not often penalized for this behavior.

and beads in their hair. They were confident. Sometimes they screamed when they scored. Much of the white audience didn't seem ready for that.

Serena said there were many times when fans would cheer if she or her sister lost. One tournament's fans called the sisters and their father racist names. In response, Venus and Serena both **boycotted** the tournament for years.

Critics also made sexist jokes about Serena's body. They compared her to a man because she was muscular. Serena struggled with these comments. But she came to embrace her powerful body.

Venus, meanwhile, fought for equal pay. She had achieved that at Wimbledon in 2007. She won the title that year. She earned the same prize money as the men's champion, Roger Federer.

The two sisters have also been role models for other Black women in tennis.

Naomi Osaka (center) said Serena's legacy will live on through all the women of color she's inspired.

In 2017, Sloane Stephens beat Madison Keys in the US Open Final. Both players are Black. The next year, Naomi Osaka won her first major. And Coco Gauff won her first in 2023. These stars were all inspired by the Williams sisters.

In 2022, Serena took time away from competing. But Venus was still competing in 2023. She was 43 years old. Both sisters had legendary careers. They were champions on the court. They inspired people both on and off the court. They were two of the best tennis players ever.

NAOMI OSAKA

Serena lost to Naomi Osaka in the 2018 US Open Final. It was **bittersweet** for Osaka. She was happy. But she also felt bad that she had beaten her hero. Osaka was 20 at the time. Serena was 36. Osaka said Serena had inspired her to start playing tennis as a young girl. She said she was happy to see a strong Black woman on TV.

VENUS WILLIAMS

- **Height:** 6 feet 1 inch (185 cm)
- **Weight:** 163 pounds (74 kg)
- **Born:** June 17, 1980
- **Birthplace:** Lynwood, California
- **Major achievements:** Wimbledon Champion (5); US Open Champion (2); Olympic Gold (1)

SERENA WILLIAMS

- **Height:** 5 feet 9 inches (175 cm)
- **Weight:** 159 pounds (72 kg)
- **Born:** September 26, 1981
- **Birthplace:** Saginaw, Michigan
- **Major achievements:** Australian Open Champion (7); French Open Champion (3); Wimbledon Champion (7); US Open Champion (6); Olympic Gold (1)

DOUBLES ACHIEVEMENTS

Australian Open Champions (4); French Open Champions (2); Wimbledon Champions (6); US Open Champions (2); Olympic Gold (3)

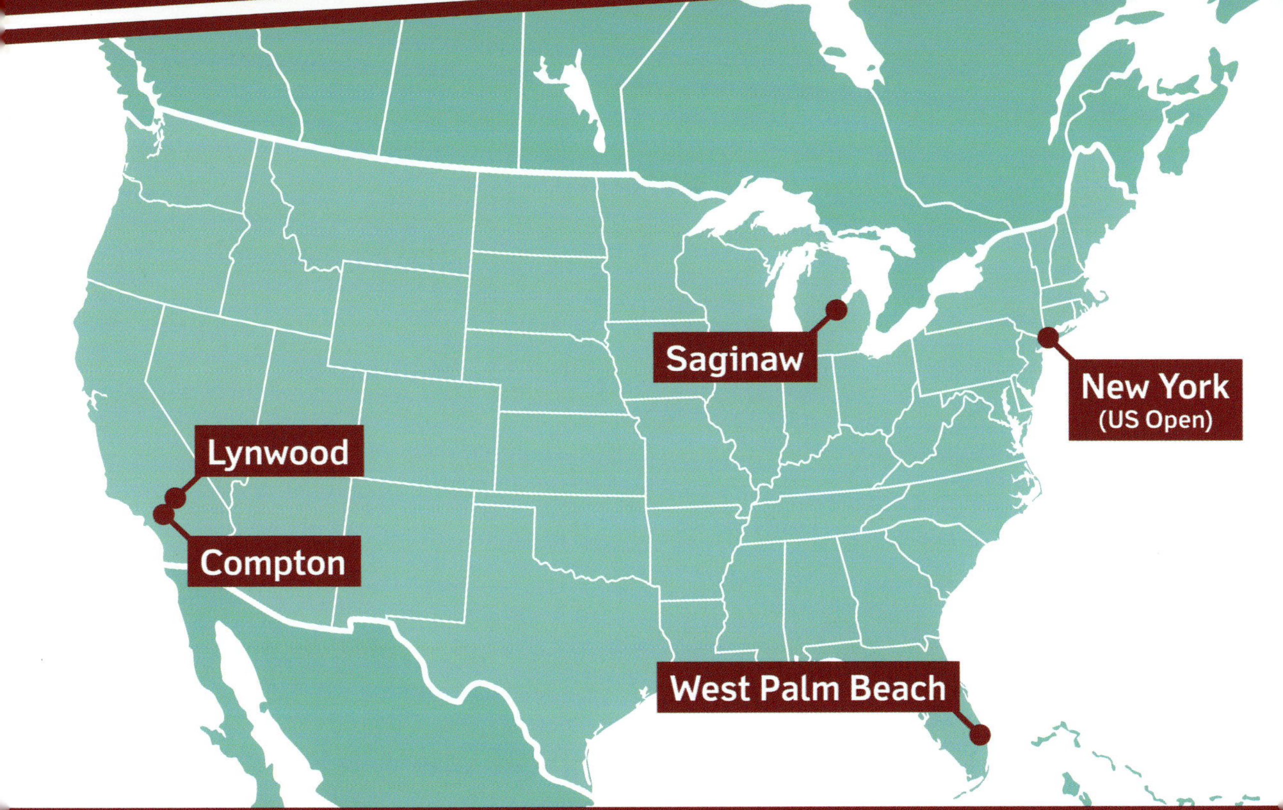

Saginaw
New York
(US Open)
Lynwood
Compton
West Palm Beach

London
(Wimbledon)
Paris
(French Open)

Melbourne
(Australian Open)

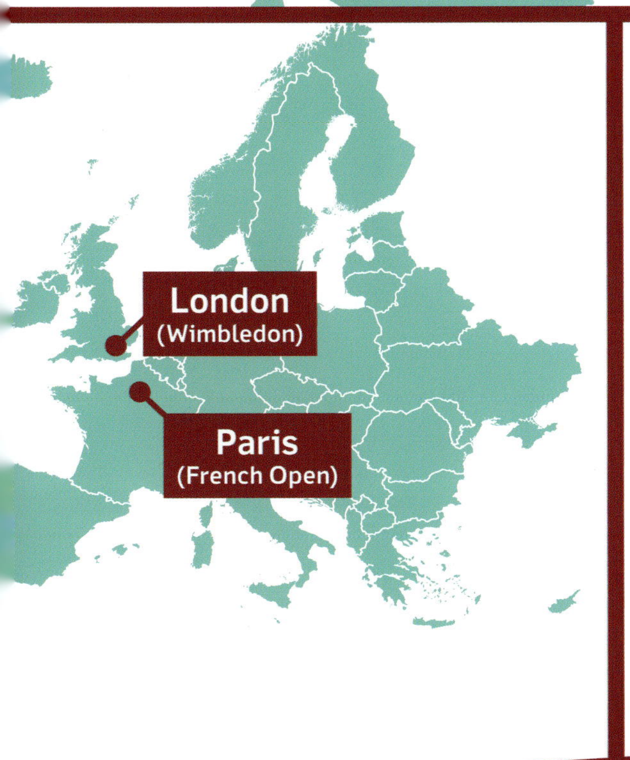

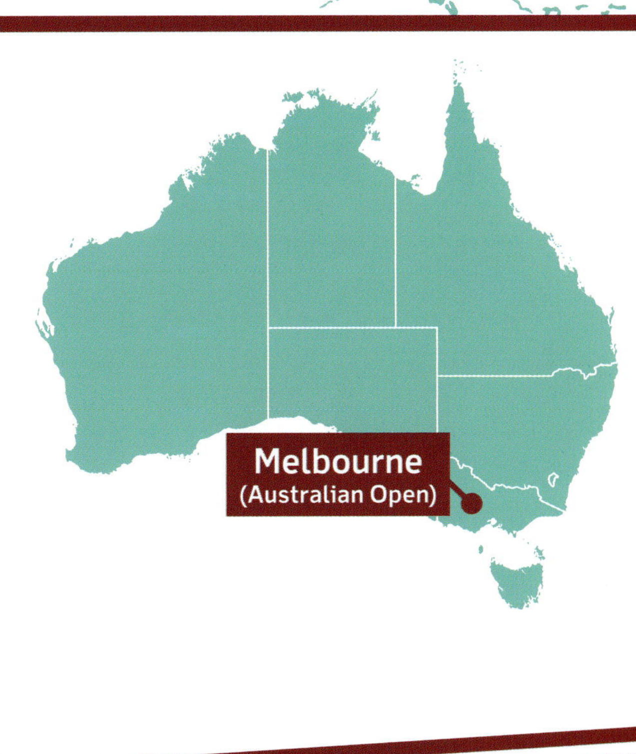

FOCUS ON

VENUS AND SERENA WILLIAMS

Write your answers on a separate sheet of paper.

1. Write a paragraph explaining the main ideas of Chapter 2.

2. If you could spend a day with Venus and Serena, what would you ask them? Why?

3. How old was Venus when she turned pro?

   A. 14 years old
   B. 18 years old
   C. 43 years old

4. Why were the tennis careers of Venus and Serena so important?

   A. They were never treated differently because of their race or gender.
   B. They inspired younger generations of players.
   C. They became popular without winning many tournaments.

Answer key on page 32.

GLOSSARY

boycotted
Refused to take part in something as a form of protest.

circuit
A series of tournaments that professional tennis players take part in.

endorsement
When athletes or celebrities get paid to use a company's product.

Grand Slam
One of the four major tennis events. They include the Australian Open, the French Open, Wimbledon, and the US Open.

Open Era
Tennis after 1968, when both pro and non-pro tennis players could play in Grand Slam tournaments.

racism
Hatred or mistreatment of people because of their skin color or ethnicity.

sexist
Having to do with hatred or mistreatment of people because of their gender.

TO LEARN MORE

BOOKS

Hewson, Anthony K. *Serena Williams.* Minneapolis: Abdo Publishing, 2024.

Scheff, Matt. *Naomi Osaka.* Mendota Heights, MN: Focus Readers, 2020.

Smith, Elliott. *Black Achievements in Sports*. Minneapolis: Lerner Publications, 2024.

NOTE TO EDUCATORS

Visit **www.focusreaders.com** to find lesson plans, activities, links, and other resources related to this title.

INDEX

Answer Key: 1. Answers will vary; **2.** Answers will vary; **3.** A; **4.** B